Lisa was waiting for her mum to come and collect her from school. It was snowing, it was raining and it was very cold.

“I bet I know what’s happened,” said Lisa to Mrs West. “I bet the car has broken down again.”

Lisa was right. At last, Mum arrived in a taxi.

"I'm sorry I'm late," she said. "The car wouldn't start again. It doesn't like this cold weather. It really is time I bought a better one."

"You can't!" said Lisa. "I like our car. It's part of the family. It would be like selling me or John." John was Lisa's brother.

"You and John are not falling to pieces," said Mum.

That evening, Mum spent a long time looking at the cars for sale in the newspaper.

"I really must buy a new car," she said, "I need one for my job."

Lisa's mum was a nurse. She was often called out to emergencies.

"There's nothing wrong with your car," said John. "It's just that you don't look after it."

But Mum had made up her mind.

"It will mean that we won't have a holiday this year," she said, "but that can't be helped."

At the weekend John, Mum, and Lisa went to the car showrooms.

There were cars of all shapes, sizes, and colours. Some of them were too expensive. Some of them were old bangers.

"I can't seem to make up my mind," said Mum.

Then Mum saw it.

"That's it!" she said. "That's the car I'm going to buy. It's just what I've been looking for."

"But it hasn't got a roof," said Lisa.

"Yes it has," said Mum. "It has a folding roof."

Mum was very excited about the new car. She went into the showroom and bought it straight away.

"Can I keep the old one?" asked John.

"Yes," said Mum. "Nobody else would want it."

Mum was very proud of her new car. She polished it until the paintwork shone like a mirror. Lisa helped her.

John worked on the old car. He spent a long time repairing the engine. Then he patched up the rusty bits, and gave it a new coat of paint. Lisa thought the old car looked as good as new.

"It's Aunt Vicky's wedding next month," said Mum. "I'll drive Aunt Vicky and Grandad to the church. You and John will have to go in the old car."

"Good," said Lisa. "I like the old car best."

On the morning of the wedding, Mum and Lisa had to go shopping in town.

"We have to collect the wedding cake," said Mum. "We'll have to hurry, we haven't much time."

Mum drove into town and parked the car in a multi-storey car park. A young man was hiding behind a pillar.

"That man looks suspicious," said Lisa. "Perhaps he's a thief."

"Don't worry," said Mum. "The car will be quite safe. Nobody steals cars from places like this. Car park attendants keep an eye on things, and there are cameras everywhere."

It didn't take Mum and Lisa long to collect the wedding cake. But when they got back to the car park there was no sign of Mum's new car.

"Oh no, the car's been stolen," said Mum. Just then a car raced past them.

"There it is! There it is!" said Mum. "That young man is driving my car away."

"I told you that man looked like a thief," said Lisa.

Mum and Lisa rushed into the street. They saw John driving down the street in the old car.

"Stop, John! Stop!" shouted Mum. "My new car has been stolen." Mum and Lisa jumped into John's car.

"Which way did he go?" asked John.

"To the left," said Mum.

"No, to the right," said Lisa.

"It's no good," said John. "We've lost him. We'd better go to the police station."

At the police station Mum spoke to the sergeant. Lisa and John had to wait while Mum filled in forms.

"Come on, Mum," said Lisa. "This is taking ages. Have you forgotten about the wedding?"

"The wedding!" groaned Mum. "We'll be late."

“Look!” shouted Lisa. “That’s the thief!” The young man they had been chasing was walking past the police station.

“Stop him!” shouted Mum, and she ran outside.

Mum ran at the young man and tackled him. They fell in a heap on the pavement.

The young man struggled but Mum held on to him.

"You stole my car," she shouted.

"No, I didn't," said the young man. "I'm a policeman!"

"I was on duty in the car park this morning," said the young man. "I was looking after the cars, not stealing them."

"But I saw you driving my car," said Mum.

"I was driving my own car," said the young man. "Come and see."

Mum, Lisa, and John went to look at the policeman's car.

"Oh," said Mum. "It's the same make and colour as my car but the number plate is different."

"Let's go back to the car park and see if we can find yours," said the policeman.

Mum's face was very red. They all got into the policeman's car and drove back to the car park.

"Why aren't you wearing a uniform?" asked Lisa.

"I'm in plain clothes," said the policeman.

There were several floors in the car park and they all looked the same.

"You see," said Mum, "there's the car we parked next to, but my car has gone."

"Let's try the next floor," said the policeman.

They walked up to the next floor. Mum's new car was there. It was parked next to a shiny blue car exactly like the one on the lower floor. This time Mum's face went really red.

"Never mind," said the policeman. "Anybody can make a mistake."

"Yes," said Mum. "I've just made another. I've left the keys of my new car at the police station."

"We'll just have to go and collect them," said John.

"Mum! The cake! Where's the cake?" said Lisa.

"Oh no," said Mum. "I left it here by mistake and now it's gone. What am I going to say to Aunt Vicky? This will spoil her wedding."

"There won't be a wedding if we don't hurry up," said John.

Back at the police station there was a big surprise.

"Is this your wedding cake?" asked the sergeant.

"Yes, it is," said Mum. "Now everything will be all right. We've just got time to get there. But we'll have to go in the old car. There isn't time to fetch the new one."

They arrived at Aunt Vicky's house just in time. Mum explained that they would all have to squash into the old car, but nobody minded. Grandad tied a ribbon on to the old car.

"I'm glad we came in the old car," said Lisa. "It looks as good as new after all the work John has put into it."

"I'm glad too," said Aunt Vicky. "This old car is like part of the family."